Creative Keyboard's

Deluxe Blues Piano Solo Book

By Matt Dennis
& Paul Smith

Creative Keyboard Publications
A Division of Mel Bay Publications, Inc.

Matt Dennis

Composer and author Matt Dennis has been a guest on a variety of TV shows and has appeared at leading clubs and concert halls throughout the country. Matt is especially recognized for his talents in the field of jazz, where his many compositions for jazz piano are legendary. His compositions include such great standards as "Angel Eyes," "Let's Get Away from It All," "Will You Still Be Mine," "The Night We Called It a Day," "Everything Happens to Me," and many more. His songs have been recorded by the Tommy Dorsey Orchestra, Frank Sinatra, Jo Stafford, Connie Haines, Tony Bennett, and many others.

Paul Smith

Well-known jazz pianist Paul Smith has been actively involved in the field of popular music for decades. Some of his accomplishments include:
Johnny Richards' band as pianist-arranger
Ozzie Nelson's band
Arranger for the Red Skelton radio show
Played with the Les Paul trio and the Andrews Sisters
Tommy Dorsey Orchestra as pianist-arranger
Rehearsal pianist at Warner Bros. studio
NBC staff pianist in Hollywood
Recorded extensively with Billy May, Paul Weston, Les Baxter, Ray Anthony, and other big bands during the '50s
Arranger-composer on many industrial films and commercials
Accompanist for almost every singer who appeared on NBC in Hollywood between 1950 and 1962
Pianist-conductor for Ella Fitzgerald, Sammy Davis Jr., Pat Boone, Steve Allen's TV show, Rosemary Clooney, Edie Adams, Joni James, Bing Crosby, and others.

In addition, Paul Smith has approximately 50 solo albums on Capitol, Verve, MGM, Imperial, Warner Bros., Discwasher, and currently records extensively on Outstanding Records, an independent company based in Huntington Beach, California. He has been a studio musician since 1950 and is currently playing, teaching, and doing studio work.

The Blues

Benny Goodman, Johnny Mercer (the fine songwriter), and myself (at the piano) were running over some songs one day, a few years ago at Capitol Records in Hollywood. One song had a certain chord progression and Benny, after hearing it, made the comment, "It's just the blues!" and proceeded to play it over on his clarinet in his wonderfully relaxed style. A short time later at a session where I had the pleasure of recording (as a singer) with Benny and his orchestra, I heard him make the same remark to his sidemen/musicians. They were having some difficulty in interpreting the beat and the phrasing of a particular arrangement. It was most enlightening to note how, after Benny's remark, the band seemed to catch the spirit, and the results were great.

In reflection, and through my own experience as a professional pianist, I can see where *playing the blues is an "attitude."* This attitude can put you in the proper relaxed mood and frame of mind necessary for playing either the written arrangement or for any natural improvisation based on the chord pattern of such an arrangement.

The blues originated after the Civil War in the sad or "sorrowful" songs of black folk music. After the turn of the century, with the influence of New Orleans jazz, the blues took on the basic 12-bar form, with a simple set of chord changes. There are solo examples of this form herein. **The blues scale** consists of the notes of the major scale with the 3rd, 5th, and 7th notes "flatted" or lowered one half step . . . the "flatted 5th" being a more recent addition. These flatted notes are traditionally called **"blue notes."**

The **12-bar blues** remains the most popular; however, new chord construction is continually introduced to support more sophisticated harmonic and melodic sounds. **Contemporary blues** can be quite uninhibited in form — rhythmically, as well. How inventive the soloist becomes improvisationally will depend upon his or her "intuitive" knowledge and "feel" of the chords used in a blues (or jazz) piece.

To the pianist, teacher, or student: For the most enjoyment of these solos, and the best results, play with a relaxed feeling. Remember, ***"It's just the blues!"***

Sincerely,
Matt Dennis

Contents

An Introduction to the Blues

Lyrics by
GINNY DENNIS a.s.c.a.p.

Music by
MATT DENNIS a.s.c.a.p.

Slow Blues
Key of A Minor (Relative minor of the key of C major)

Am Am7/Gbass F E7
There, on the ta - ble, you left a lit - tle note.
Am Dm Am
I start - ed
Dm E7
cry - in' as I read what you wrote.
Am Dm Am
You said you
2ND CHORUS:
Am (E7) A Bass Am7 (D7) Dm7
hat - ed to tell me, but you were leav - in' town.
Back-beat bass accent
Am Dm Am (add 6th) Am7

Am7
(E7)
A Bass
Am7
(D7)
Dm E7(9th)
No long - er loved me,
and could - n't hang a - round.
F7(9th)
B Bass
E7(9th)
NC
Am
(E7)
A Bass
Am7
(D7)
Dm7
You took my lov - in'
and, Ba - by, I've got news;
Am
Dm
A Bass
Am(add6th)
Am7
There's on - ly
B7(+5)
E7
A7
one thing that you
left me, "AN IN - TRO -
rall.
dim
D7
G7
G♯dim Am
(D)
L. H.
R. H.
(Entire blues chord opt. 8va)
DUC - TION TO THE BLUES".
play slowly
Pedal

Lonesome Mornin' Blues

By MATT DENNIS a.s.c.a.p.

Note: When the **beat** is fairly established in the R.H. melody by the syncopated notation, the L.H. can play a sustained interval or chord accompaniment (as above). Just be sure to keep the *regular beat count* going steadily.

Original Blues in B♭

The 12-Bar Blues

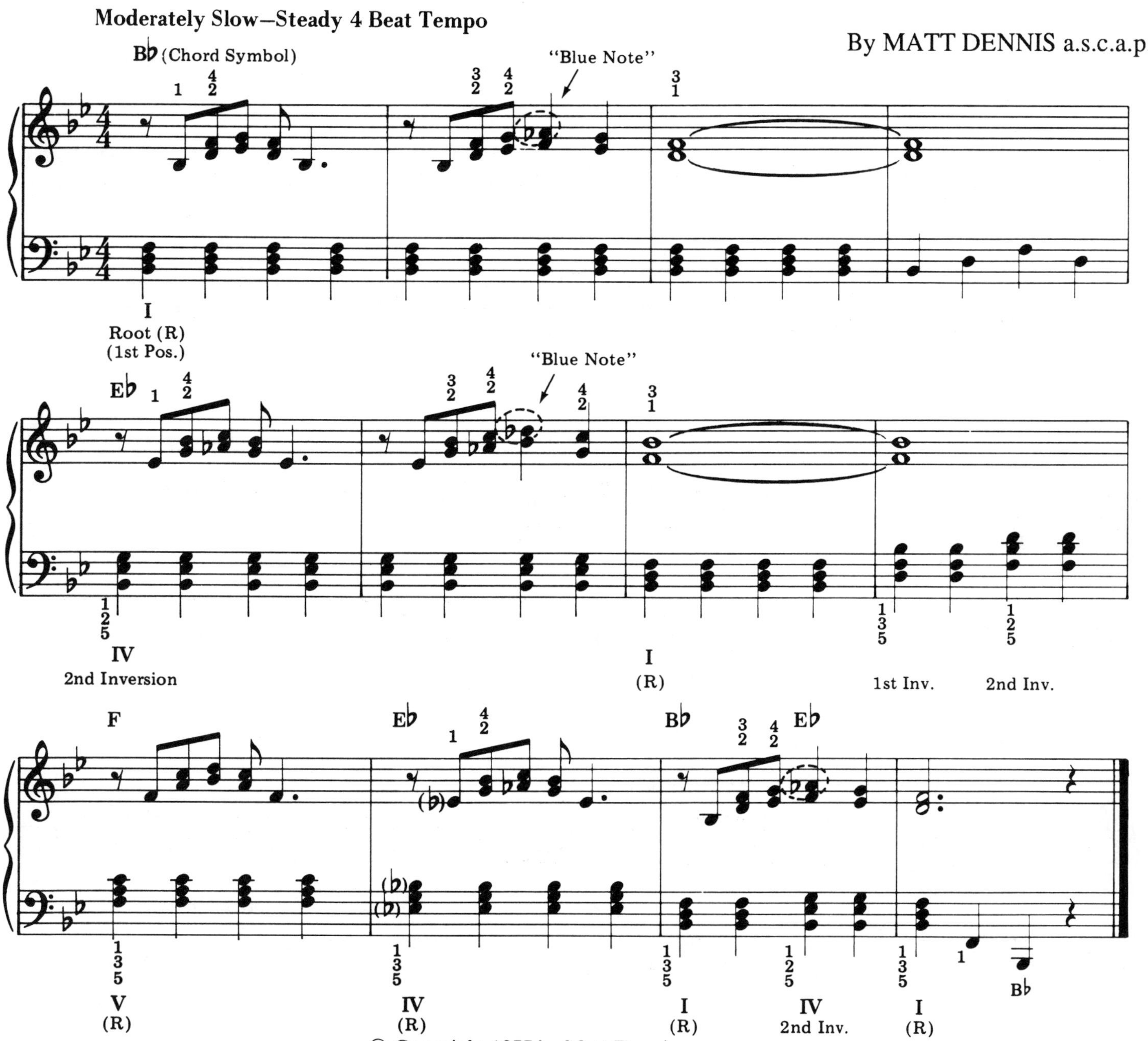

Chord symbols = names of the fundamental **chords** used in each measure, whether in the bass clef, treble clef (in the melodic structure), or in a combination of the notes in **both** clefs. You will run across this in most popular music. Some pianists *with a full knowledge of chord harmonies* can read a melody from the sheet music and play the proper harmony with interesting **inversions** of the chords, just by reading the chord symbols. Your playing can have more individual style when you do this . . . it is an enjoyable experience and certainly a worthwhile goal. *Become familiar with chord inversions in various keys.*

"Blue Note" = a flatted note, characteristic of the blues.

Boogie Woogie on the Blues

The exciting and very popular boogie woogie rhythm. Both hands play **dotted eighth and sixteenth notes** with a steady beat.

By MATT DENNIS a.s.c.a.p.

G7th chord: Actually, the chord is only "implied" here.

Sleepwalkin' Blues

1st Chorus: The melody is strong and moving; the left hand plays the *added 6th* and introduces the *added 9th and augmented 9th (♯9) notes*.

2nd Chorus: A variation of the original melody based on chords used; has an "improvised" sound and feeling. The back-beat bass in the 5th and 6th bars gives a surprising rhythmic effect with the accent on the *2nd and 4th* beats instead of the usual 1st and 3rd. Note the *added 9ths* in the 8th bar and the natural blues ending.

Easy Blues Tempo

By MATT DENNIS a.s.c.a.p.

C
C
C7
F7
Back-beat bass
C
G7+
C7 add9
B♭7add9
A7add9
9th
9th
9th
Dm
F
(F♯dim7)
C/Gbass
G7
C
rit.

I Got the Blues for St. Louis

Moderately with a Beat

Lyrics and Music by
MATT DENNIS a.s.c.a.p.

F C7/G F/A nc
C7(9)sus
(no 3rd add 4th a "suspension")
To Coda
I had a gal in St. Lou - is
un - til my sweet ba - by clipp'd me
If there's good news in St. Lou - is . . .
G7 C7(9)sus
1. F Bb6 B♮dim7 F/Cbass
no chord
done turn'd me down. I fell in
off - a her
2. F Bb/Fbass F Bb/Fbass F
F F7/Eb
vine.
Oh, Me!
mf
no Bb
Bb9/D
no Bb
Bbm9/Db
F/C Ddim7 C7/E
Oh, My!
She's as pret - ty as can be.

F7
Fm
Fm7
no Bb
Bb9/D
no Bb
Bbm9/Db
Oh, Me!
Oh, My!
L.H. "fill"
F/C
Ddim7
C7/E
F
She's as pret - ty as can be
Won - der
"fill"
C7
no G
*G9b5/Bbass
C7
** no Db no C no C
Db7 C7/E F7/Eb
why that sweet gal
brought me all that mis - e - ry.
F7/A
Bb
Db7/B
F/C
Bb/Cbass
no chord
D.S. al Coda
(Back to Sign 𝄋)
I'm go - in'
f
mp
sf
mp

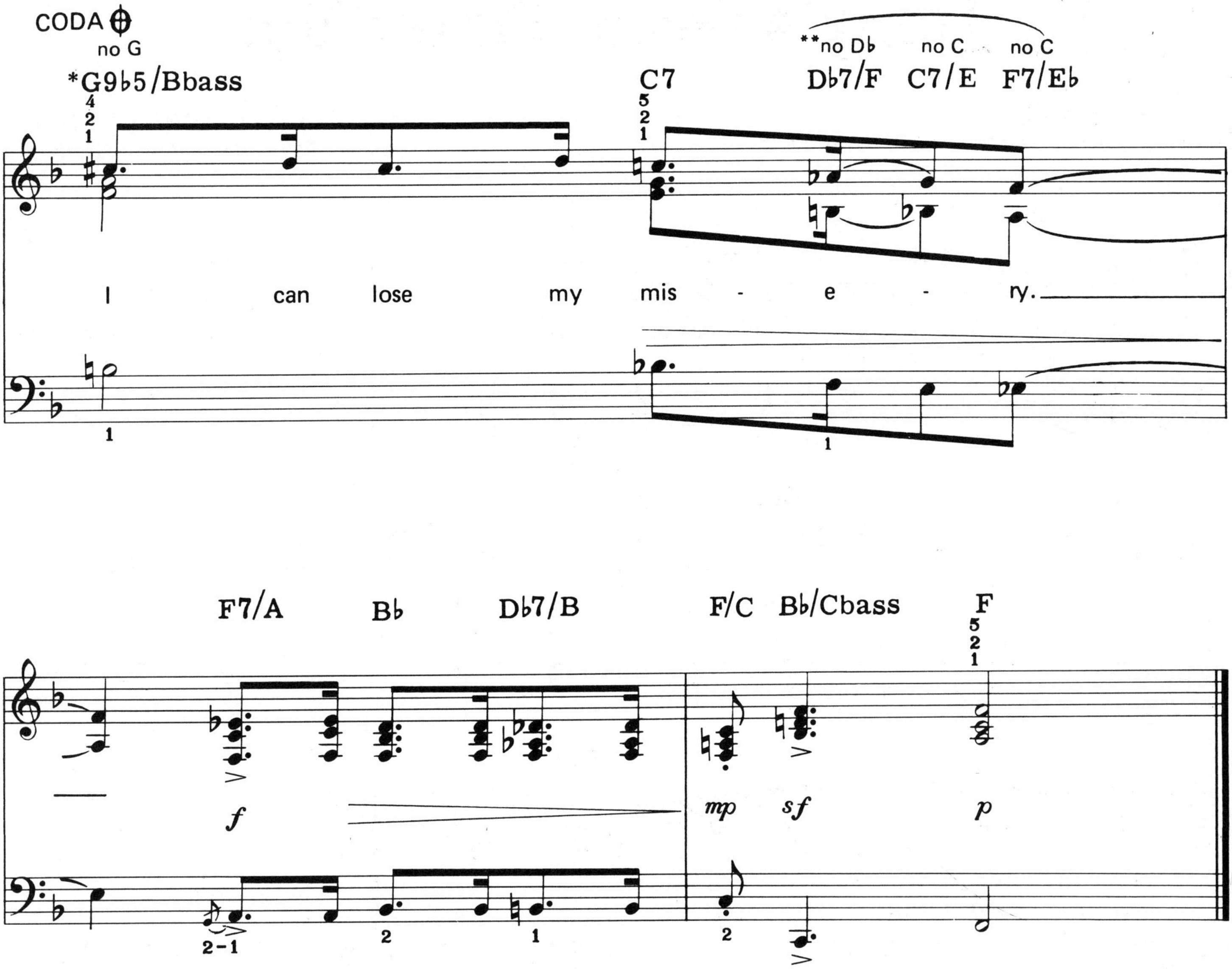

As you may have noticed, we are getting into more involved and sophisticated **chords.** There is not space for great detail on such chords; however, specific ones in the blues piece above are explained as follows:

*The **G9♭5 with the B bass** is a rich-sounding chord based on the G7th. The 5th note of the G scale is flatted ½ step, making the ♭5. We use a B bass instead of the usual G (tonic) note due to the position and voicing of that particular chord. The G is not necessary in this case, while the chord is still recognizable as a G9♭5 . . . there are enough other notes of the chord to identify it.

**The above holds good also for the chords of D♭7/F bass, C7/E bass, and the F7/E♭ bass (the C note is deleted in the latter chord), C being the 5th note of the C major scale. Due to the way in which these chords are played in sequence, the sound is fine without those notes mentioned.

Chords are fun and inspiring. Get involved!

Baby's Gone Good-Bye

Slow Blues, Sadly
Key of D minor (8-bar blues with 8-bar extension)

Lyrics by GINNY DENNIS a.s.c
Music by MATT DENNIS a.s.c.

Dave's Boogie

Boogie Woogie Blues

Moderato with a Beat

By MATT DENNIS a.s.c.a.p.

D
C
G
(D7)
G
opt. 8va
etc.
G
G7

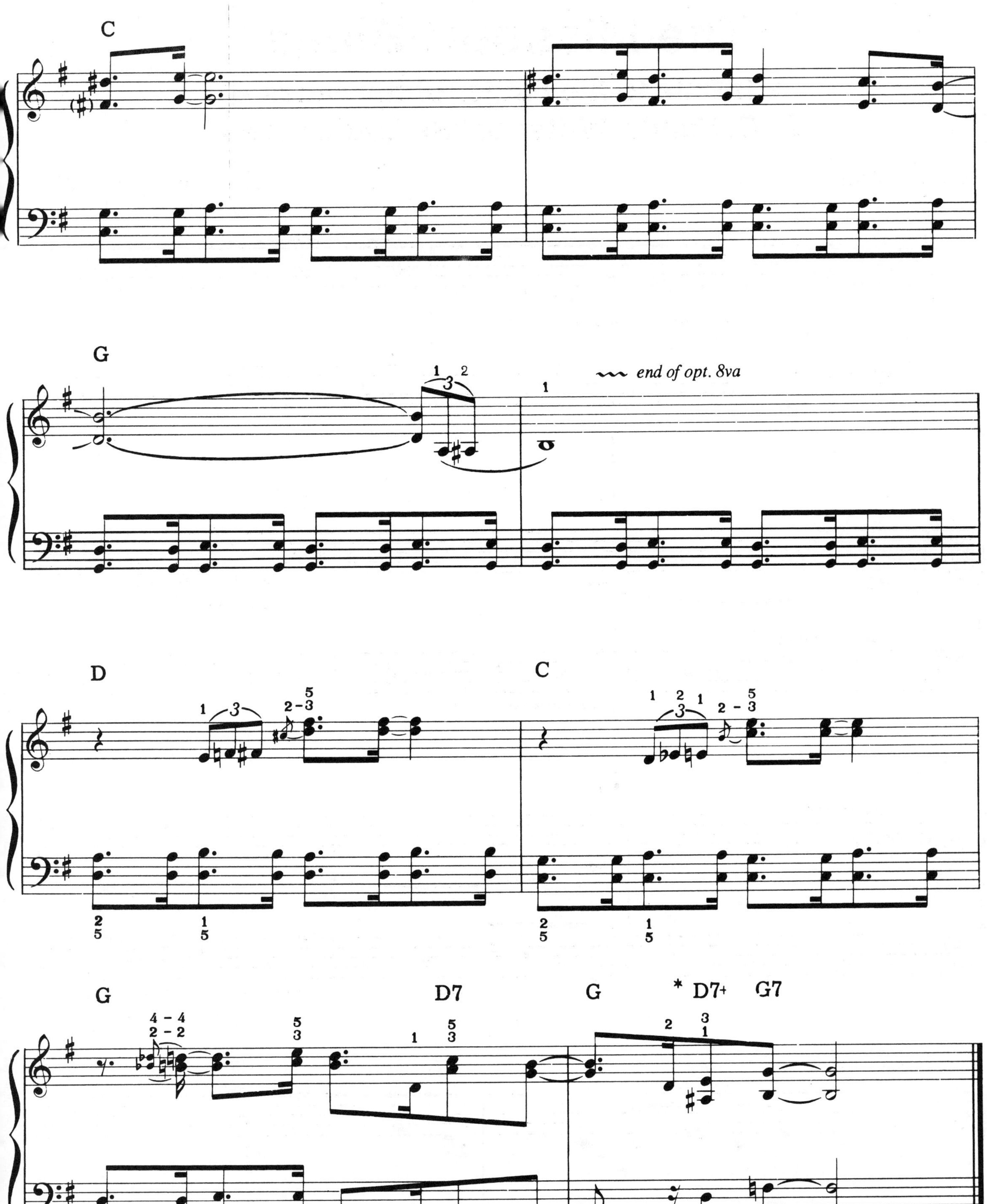

*The chord symbol for *D7th with augmented 5th* (to **augment** a note means to raise the note ½ step), the 5th note of the D7th chord being A. Raise that note to A♯.

The Missouri Blues

A Tribute to the Father of the Blues — W. C. Handy, Writer of "St. Louis Blues"

Easy Steady Beat

Composed and Arranged by
MATT DENNIS a.s.c.a.p.

F
B♭
F
F
B♭7
F
mf
F7
B♭7
F
C7
G7
C7
F
B♭7
F
rit.
mp

New Orleans

Relaxed Dixie 2-Beat Blues

Composed and Arranged by
MATT DENNIS a.s.c.a.p.

B♭ NC Dm7 G7 Dm9/A G7♭9/B♮
C7 C dim C7 NC
D. C. al Coda
CODA
Gm7 C7 A+7 A7
D7♭9 D7 Gm7 Am7 A♭dim Gm7
(Gm7) C7sus C7♭9 F B♭7 F
8va

True Blue Blues

Slowly with a Steady Beat

Composed and Arranged by
MATT DENNIS a.s.c.a.p.

Bb Bb7/D Eb7 E dim
mf
Bb/F F7sus Bbmaj7/F Bb7sus Bb7 Eb7 Bbm7
Eb7 E dim Bb/F Ab7 G7 F/A Bbm G7/B
Cm7 C#dim Bb/D Ebm C7/E♮ F7sus
Bb Bb7/D Eb E dim Bb/F F7+(+9) Bb9
(opt. 8va - - - -)
opt. rit.
(opt. 8va - - - -)

Oh Yeah!
A Tribute to Louis Armstrong

Medium Blues Tempo

Composed and Arranged by
MATT DENNIS a.s.c.a.p.

Eb7
Break
E dim
NC
Bb
3
Fm6/D
G7
1. C7
F7 add 6
(trill)
Bb
(F7)
NC
(Cm7/G)
(F7/A)
2. C7
F7 add 6
Fm6/D
G7
C7
F7 add 6
(trill)
Bb
F7+(+9)
Bb9 add 6
slight pause
"OH YEAH!"

Muddy Blues

Slow and Steady Blues

Composed and Arranged by
MATT DENNIS a.s.c.a.p.

(In My) Melancholy Mood

A Blues-Ballad Rhapsody

Composed and Arranged by
MATT DENNIS a.s.c.a.p.

Ad Lib (Out of Tempo)

Verse

Notes in brackets — optional

To Coda
NC (F bass) Fmaj9 C/E Ab7/Eb Dm7 G7sus G7
1. C D9b5 D9 G7b9 add 6 G9+
accel.
(opt.
)
rall.
2. C Db Cmaj9 (C7 add 6) (C7+) NC
Fmaj7 E7+ E7 Am G7sus G7
Cmaj7 C7sus C7b5 Fmaj7 E7 add 6 E7/G♯ Am Am7
cresc. (build)
mf

D. S. al Coda
D7sus
D9
G7 add 6
G+7
(♭9)
dim.
poco rit.
CODA
NC
(E bass)
Em7
Am add 4
A♭dim
Gm7
C7sus
C7♭9/E
mf
(E)
Fm7
A♭ add 9
Fm6/D
poco rit.
NC
(C bass)
Cmaj9
Fmaj9
(G bass)
mp
a tempo
NC
(C bass)
Cmaj9
G7+(+9)
NC
(C bass)
Cmaj9
Fmaj9
(G bass)
NC
(C bass)
Cmaj9
G7+(+9)
Cmaj9 add 6
rall.
slowly dim.
rit.
p

Goin' Out There Tonight!

Moderate Blues Tempo

Composed and Arranged by
MATT DENNIS a.s.c.a.p.

NC
F7+9
NC
cresc.
opt.
f
D♭9
Gm7/C
NC
gradual cresc.
mf
F7+9(add 11)
play as reverse arp.
opt.
f
play together
Ped.

Early Mornin' Blues

Moderate Blues

Composed and Arranged by
MATT DENNIS a.s.c.a.p.

G D7 G D7
G D7 G9 NC
(opt. - - - - - - -)
C7 G7 C7 G7
G Am7 B♭dim G7 G♭7 F7 E7 A7
"Roll"
f
Play straight
mf
passing tones
D7sus D7 (F♯bass) G G7 (B bass) C (C♯bass) NC G/D bass D7 G
f
p
8va

Boogie Woogie Blues

Note: To correctly play the boogie beat — the **dotted eighth note** has the same value as an eighth note tied to a sixteenth note. The dot after a note adds ½ the value of the note.

This example:

Sounds the same as:

Introducing three of the most famous left-hand boogie patterns! Optional: Notes in brackets, and top notes of all L.H. intervals. The term "Vamp" applies to a 2- or 4-measure section where a rhythm pattern is introduced which may continue in the chorus to follow.

Steady Boogie Beat

Composed and Arranged by
MATT DENNIS a.s.c.a.p.

Vamp (Boogie Rhythm Pattern No. 1)

1st Chorus

C
(C7)
G
D
C
G
(D7)
NC
Vamp (Boogie Rhythm Pattern No. 2)
G
These harmonic intervals are called "10ths."
2nd Chorus
G

G7
C
G
D
C
G
D7
(D7)
G NC
opt.
Vamp (Boogie Rhythm Pattern No. 3)
G
3rd Chorus
G7
mp

C7
G
D7
mf
C7
G7
D
f
C
G
D7
G
D7+
G7
Play as is

Blues for Dad

Moderate Blues Tempo

Composed and Arranged by
MATT DENNIS a.s.c.a.p.

D♭6/E♭
NC
F bass
B♭
A♭6/B♭
NC
F bass
B♭
A♭6/B♭
NC
F bass
F9
E♭/F
NC
F bass
E♭9
D♭/E♭
NC
F bass
B♭
A♭6/B♭
NC
F bass
B♭
A♭6/B♭
NC
F bass

Bb
Ab6/Bb
NC
F bass
mf
8va
Bb
Ab6/Bb
NC
F bass
Bb (7)
8va
8va
Ab6/Bb
NC
F bass
3
Bb7
Ab6/Bb
NC
Eb7
Db6/Eb
NC
Bb bass
Eb7
Db6/Eb
NC
F bass
3
3

B♭
A♭6/B♭
NC
F bass
B♭
8va
8va
A♭6/B♭
NC
F bass
F9
cresc.
opt.
(A)
(F)
E♭/F
NC
F bass
E♭9
D♭/E♭
NC
F bass
opt.
(G)
gradual dim.
B♭
A♭6/B♭
NC
F bass
B♭
8va
8va
A♭6/B♭
C9
F9+5
B♭9
rit.
(C)
(B♭)
mp

Livin' with the Blues

Slow Blues

Composed and Arranged by
MATT DENNIS a.s.c.a.p.

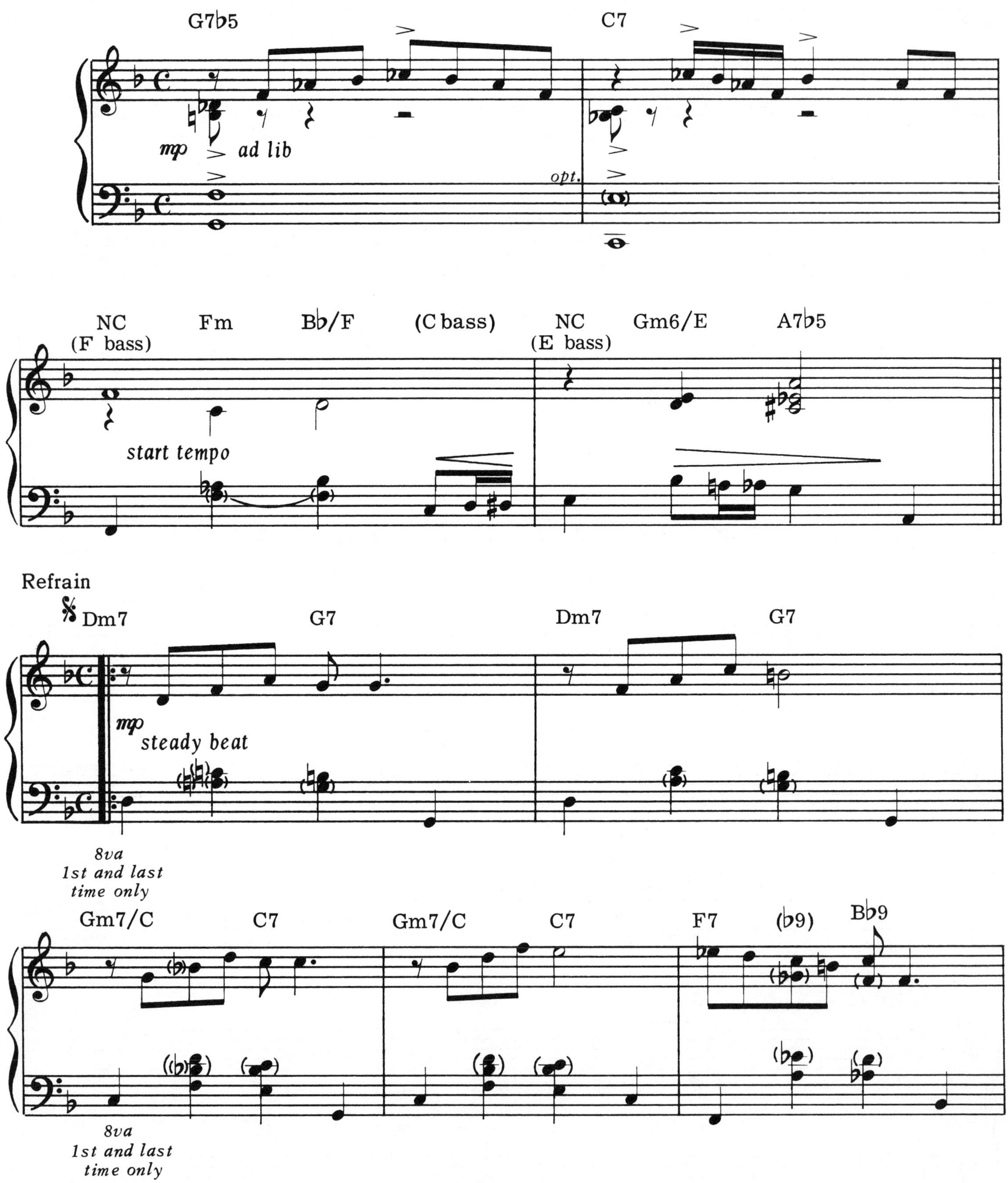

Eb7
Eb7b9
Ab7
G7b5
C7
To Coda
1.
NC
(F bass)
Fm
Bb/F
(C bass)
NC
(F bass)
Fm
Bb/F
(C bass)
2.
NC
(F bass)
Fm
Bb/F
(C bass)
NC
(E bass)
Gm6/E
A7+
A7
Dmaj7
Em7
Dmaj9/F#
Gm7
C7b5
gradual cresc.

Fm7
Bb7
E9b5
Ebmaj7
Dm7
G7
dim.
Cmaj7
Dm7
Em7
Fm7
NC
gradual cresc.
Bb7sus
Bb9
NC
A7sus
A9
D. S. al Coda
CODA
NC (F bass)
Fm
Bb/F
(C bass)
NC (F bass)
Fm
Bb/F
(C bass)
Fm7(13)
rall.
1
2

Feelin' the Pain

Steady Blues, with Expression

Composed and Arranged by
MATT DENNIS a.s.c.a.p.

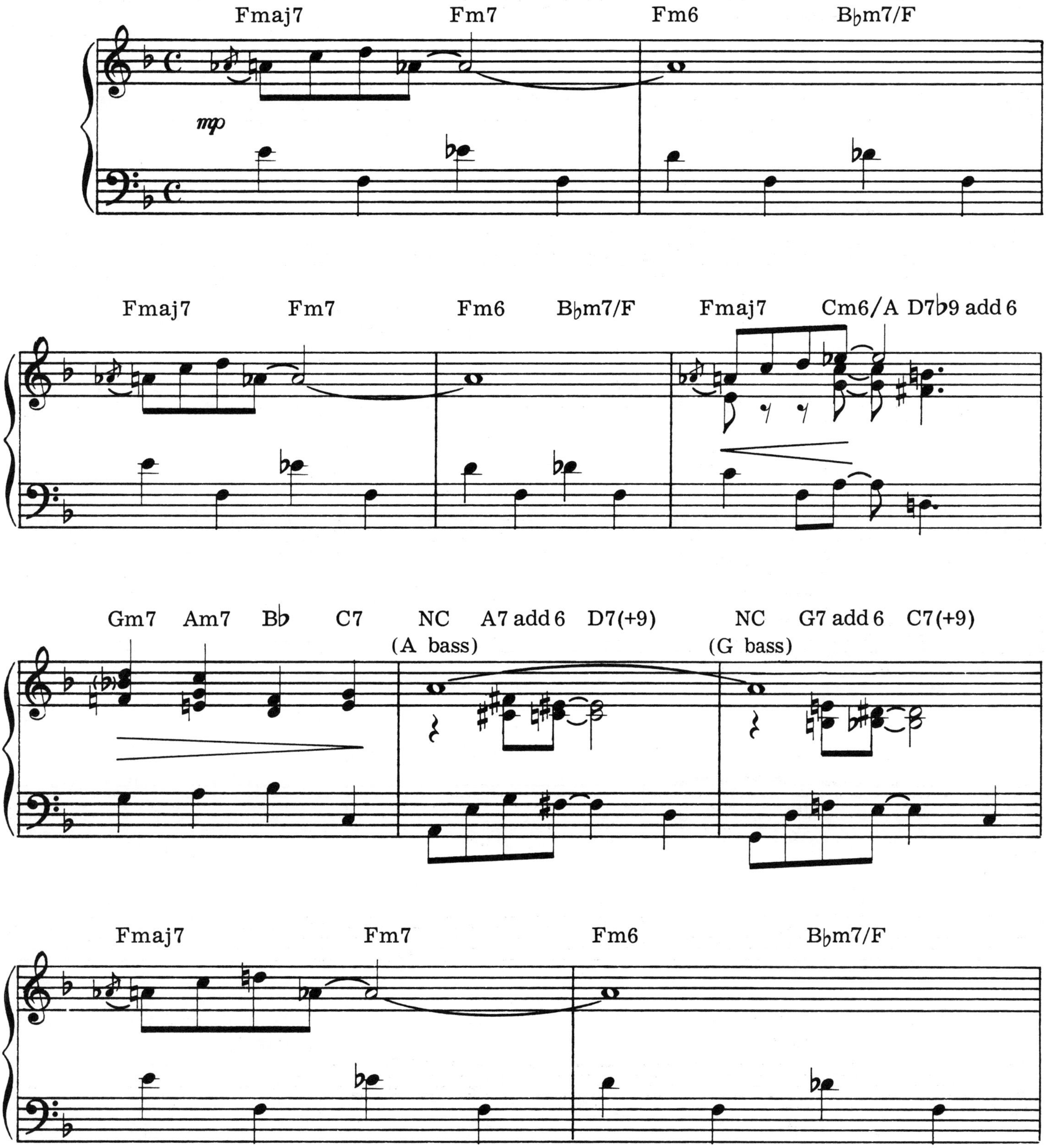

Fmaj7
Fm7
Fm6
B♭m7/F
Fmaj7
Cm6/A
D7♭9 add 6
Gm7
Am7
G7♭5
C7sus No D
opt.
NC (F bass)
Fmaj7 add D
Fm7 add D♭
(C bass)
NC (F bass)
Fmaj7
Cm9/F
cresc.
dim.
B♭
B♭m7
F
D♭7
(A♭ bass)
Gm7
Gm7/C
F
F7
Cm7/G add 4
F7/A
B♭
A7
A♭7 add 6
G7

Cmaj7
D7♭9
Dm7/G
C
B♭maj7
Am7
Gm7
f
dim.
Fmaj7
Fm7
Fm6
B♭m7/F
Fmaj7
Fm7
mp
Fm6
B♭m7/F
Fmaj7
Cm6/A
D7♭9 add 6
Gm7
Am7
B♭m7
E♭9 add 6
mf
slight rit.
NC
F
Gm7
A♭6
NC
G
A♭6
B♭
a tempo
mp
cresc.
top notes opt.
F/C
C7+(9)
F9
rit.
mf
Broadly
opt.

Wonder Where My Baby Is Tonight

Slow Blues Ballad

Lyrics by
GINNY DENNIS a.s.c.a.p.

Composed and Arranged by
MATT DENNIS a.s.c.a.p.

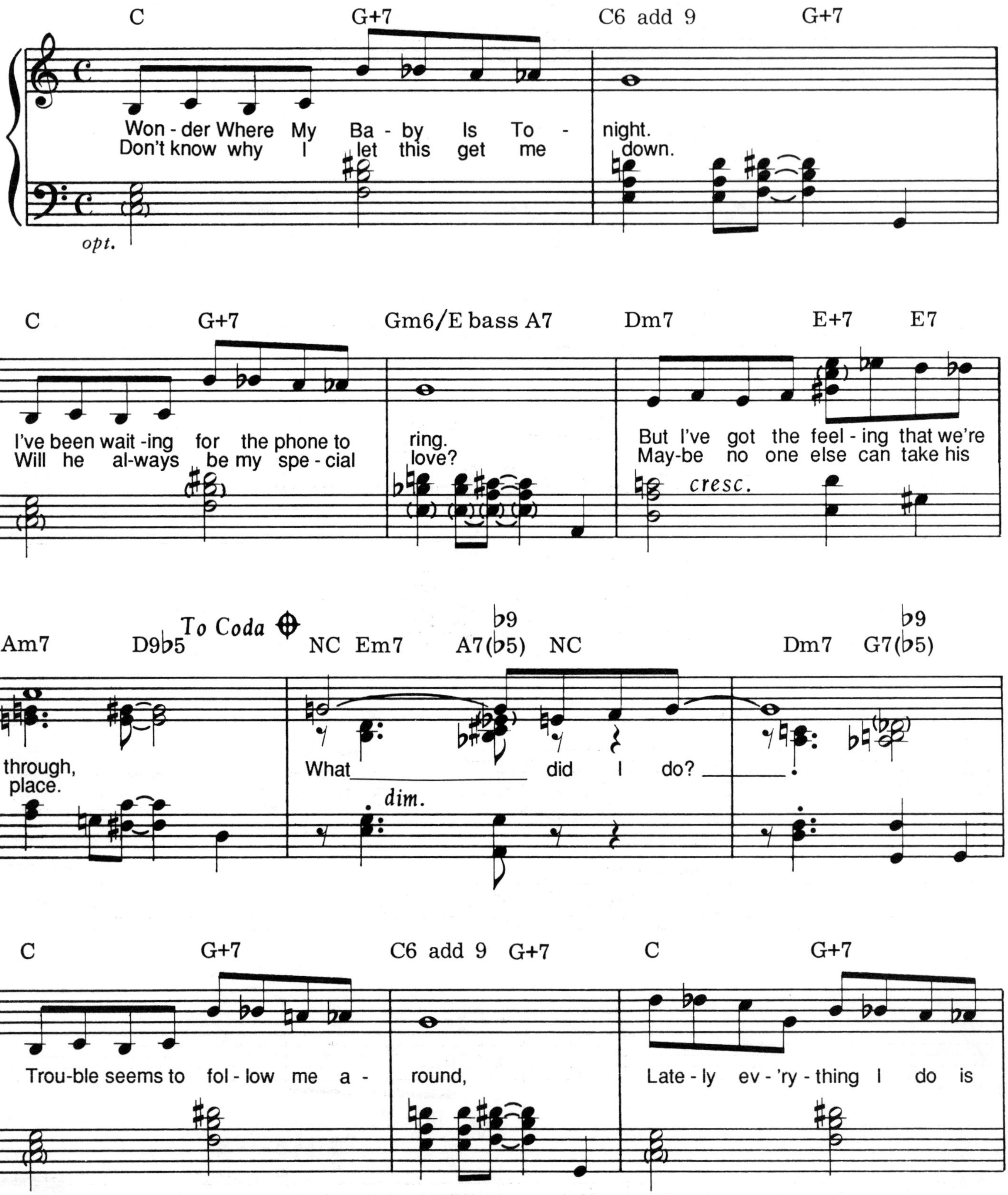

Gm6/E A7 Dm7 E+7 3 E7
wrong. May - be it's the kind of mood I'm
cresc.
Am7 D7♭5 NC Em7 Dm7 Gm9 C7♭9
in, Can't seem to win.
8va
F add 9 F Fm6
mf
My fool - ish heart keeps re - peat - ing his name,
Cmaj9/E G+7 C7 (9)
O - ver and o - ver a - gain,
Fm add 9 Fm Fm6
I watch the clock as the time hur - ries by.

D. C. al Coda
Em7 A+7 Dm7 G+7
Hop - ing he'll call Hop - ing that's all.
dim.
CODA
NC Gmaj7 G6 NC Gm7 Gm6 NC
How could they be what this guy's
gradually diminish
Fmaj7 F6 NC Fm7 Fm6
been to me?
NC Em7 A7(♭5) ♭9 NC Dm7 G7(♭5) ♭9 NC C6 add 9
I want him back in my arms.
dim.
rit.
8va
Cmaj9
slowly
Won - der Where My Ba - by Is To - night.
p
8va

Big Band Blues

Five lively choruses arranged to convey the pulse of the **big band** playing an instrumental blues arrangement. Each chorus builds in sequence to the strong ending.

There is an optional *Fine* ending for a four-chorus arrangement, should you wish to play the fifth chorus as a separate solo in itself— a study in "block chord" playing of the blues. If the arrangement is done in its entirety, the fifth chorus is the equivalent of the final "ensemble" chorus a big band would play.

The "unison-riff" ideas shown in the treble clef in the first four choruses would be played by the band, or possibly replaced with original improvised solo instrumental choruses (piano, trumpet, sax, etc.), all leading up to the last ensemble band chorus and effective ending.

The fun thing about playing this blues arrangement is that you can substitute improvised right-hand ideas indefinitely for any of the four choruses — just keep your left-hand rhythm patterns constant, as written. Try it!

Moderately Fast Blues

Opt. ending at Fine, or continue to Special Ensemble Chorus

F
Gm7
C7 (sus)
F
NC
2
F
F7
B♭7
F
Gm7

C7 (sus)
F
NC
3
F
mf
F7
B♭7
F
Gm7
C7
F
Gm7/C bass
slight cresc.

4
F
F7
B♭7
F
Gm7
For opt. ending, play FINE
C7 (sus)
NC
(opt.)
opt.
(F)
F7/A
B♭
D♭7/B
F/C
Fmaj9
FINE
f
rit.

To continue:
F/C
C7sus
mp
Special Ensemble Chorus
Play broadly
opt. — may be played half as fast, in 4/4
opt. — may be played as an individual blues
5
Fmaj7
F7/A
B♭9♭5 add 6
B♭9/D
Emaj9
Fmaj9
mp Steady Beat
(F7)
NC
B♭9♭5/D add 6
B♭9
A♭7 add 6
G7♭5
mf
B6/C♯ F♯
Fmaj9
NC
Gm7 add 4
C7sus
mf
B♭m9
E♭9 add 6
Emaj9/G♯
Fmaj9/A
F9
mf
rit.
slowly

'S About Time!

Moderately

Composed and Arranged by
MATT DENNIS a.s.c.a.p.

B♭7
E♭/B♭
E♭7/B♭
A♭7add6
Tacet
G7
A♭7
Tacet
E7
F7
E7
3
F7
E7
F7
D. S. al Coda
Tacet
mf
Coda
A♭
A
B♭
Tacet
F9/A
B♭7+A♭
E♭9/G
G7+/F
F7sus
B♭
f

Guess What!

Moderately Bright

Composed and Arranged by
MATT DENNIS a.s.c.a.p.

Fine last time only
Broadly — keep steady beat
poco cresc.
mp
f
dim.
D. C. al Fine

Blues for Breakfast

Slowly, with a Beat

Lyrics by
JERRY GLADSTONE

Music by
MATT DENNIS a.s.c.a.p.

11
no___ cal - o - ries.____ There's noth - ing like a long and sleep - less
Fm9 Fm7 Bb7-9 Bb7-9-5 Eb6 Abm6 EbMaj7 Fm6 (D bass) G7-5
mp
legato
14
night_____ to make you lose_____ your ap - pe - tite._____ If
Cm6(add9) D7+ D7 EbMaj7
17
an - y - thing can real - ly spoil your day_____ it's when your love_____ goes on her (his)
Bb7-9+5 Eb6(add9) Abm6 EbMaj7 Fm6 G7-5 Cm6(add9) A7+ A7

20
way.
Some
good morn-ing
C7(D bass)
D7-9+5
Gm6(add9)
mf
a tempo
A7+
D7-9+5
23
3
this
one has
been;
I
find
the
world
a -
Gm9
Gm7
C7-9
3
Fm6(add9)
26
round me
is
cav - ing
in.
She
(He)
G7+
C7-9+5
Fm9
Fm7
B♭7-9
mp

29
left me with the dawn for parts un - known, and so it's Blues for
Bb7-9 +5 Eb6 (add9) Abm6 Eb Maj7 (D bass) Fm6 G7-5 C7-9 +5 Cm9(F bass) F7-9(add6)
a tempo
32
Break-fast a - lone.
Eb9 D7-9 Gm7 Gm6 Gm7 Gm6
2nd time only
35
Repeat and gradually fade
Gm7 Gm6 Gm7 Gm6 Gm7 Gm6 Gm7 Gm6

We've Reached the Point of No Return

Slow Blues Tempo

Words and Music by
GINNY DENNIS and MATT DENNIS

7
told me that you loved__ me and I hoped that you'd be true, But
Bb BbMaj7 Bb7 Eb7 Bb
9
there's no turn - in' back,___ I know we're through.
F C7 F7
11
We've Reached the Point_______ of No Re - turn,_______ the point where
F7 Bb Bb7 Eb Cm7
mp – mf

13
love no long - er burns. You say it's
F7
B♭
F7
15
best that we should part al - tho' you
B♭
B♭ 7
E♭
Cm7
17
know it breaks my heart. I'm sor - ry, dear, if I should
F7
B♭
E♭6
B♭
E♭

20
cry, but it's so hard___ to say good - bye. A fool_ am
B♭ C7 Gm7 C7 F9 F7
23
I,___ too late__ I learned,___ We've Reached the
B♭ B♭7 E♭ Cm7
25
1. 2.
Point___ of No Re - turn, We've Reached the turn.
F7 B♭ E♭6 B♭ F7 B♭

No-Name Blues

Easy — Steady Jazz Beat

Composed and Arranged by
MATT DENNIS a.s.c.a.p.

Used by permission.

no G♭
G♭9/B♭
no F
Fmaj9/A
Dm7
no G
G7-9add6/F
no C
C7+9,-13
F6/D
G7-9add6
C+7+9
F6
no C-9
Cm7/B♭
F7−9/A
no C
Cm9/E♭
F+7/E♭
no B♭
B♭m9/D♭
B♭m6
D♭
Fmaj7/C
B♭m7
C6
Dm7
no G
G7-9/F
no C
C7/E
no F
F6/D
F Bass
F9add6/A
no F
F+7-9addG♯/A
A Bass
no B♭
B♭m9/A♭
B♭Bass
no F
Fmaj9/A
nc
B♭Bass
B♭m7
Am7
nc
A♭Bass
A♭m7
Gm7
nc
G♭Bass
G♭maj7
Fmaj7
A7-9
-5

Dm
no G
Gm6/E
A7-9
add13
A+7-9 Dm9
nc
no G
G9-5/B
no B♭
B♭m9/A♭
no B
B♭m6add
maj7
G
nc
B Bass
C Bass
no F
F/A
C Bass
Fø
nc
C Bass
C7sus4
nc
C Bass
G♭maj7
nc
A♭6
G7
G♭maj7
F
F9+11

Accents

Composed and Arranged by
PAUL SMITH

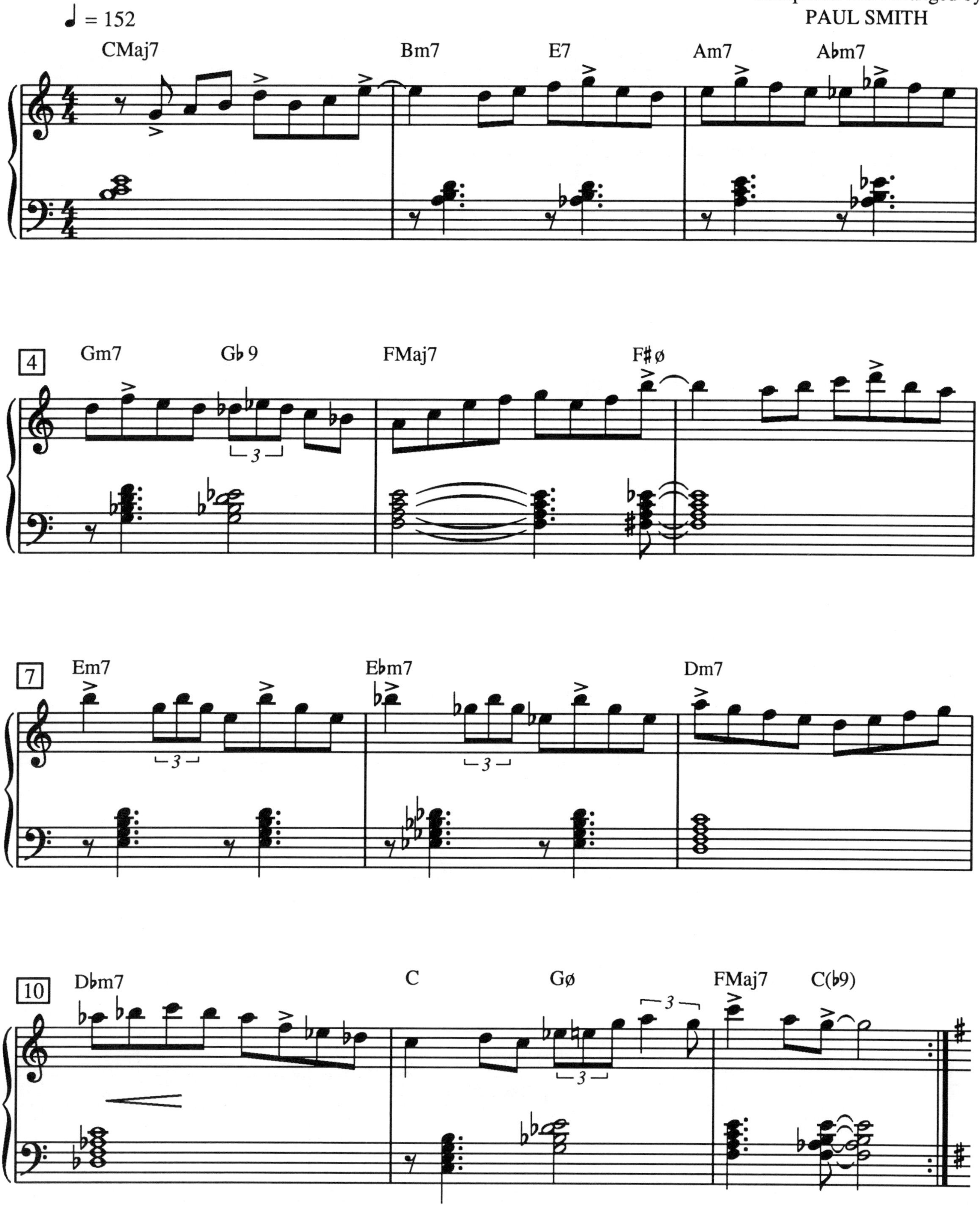

(Max.♩ = 168; practice at ♩ = 144)

25
28
31
34

Rock Comp

Composed and Arranged by
PAUL SMITH

♩ = 84 𝄋

9
G
F
C(add9)
to Coda
12
14
F(add9)
16
C(add9)
G
18
D. S. al Coda
CODA

Funky Punky

Composed and Arranged by
PAUL SMITH

13
16
19
8vb
22

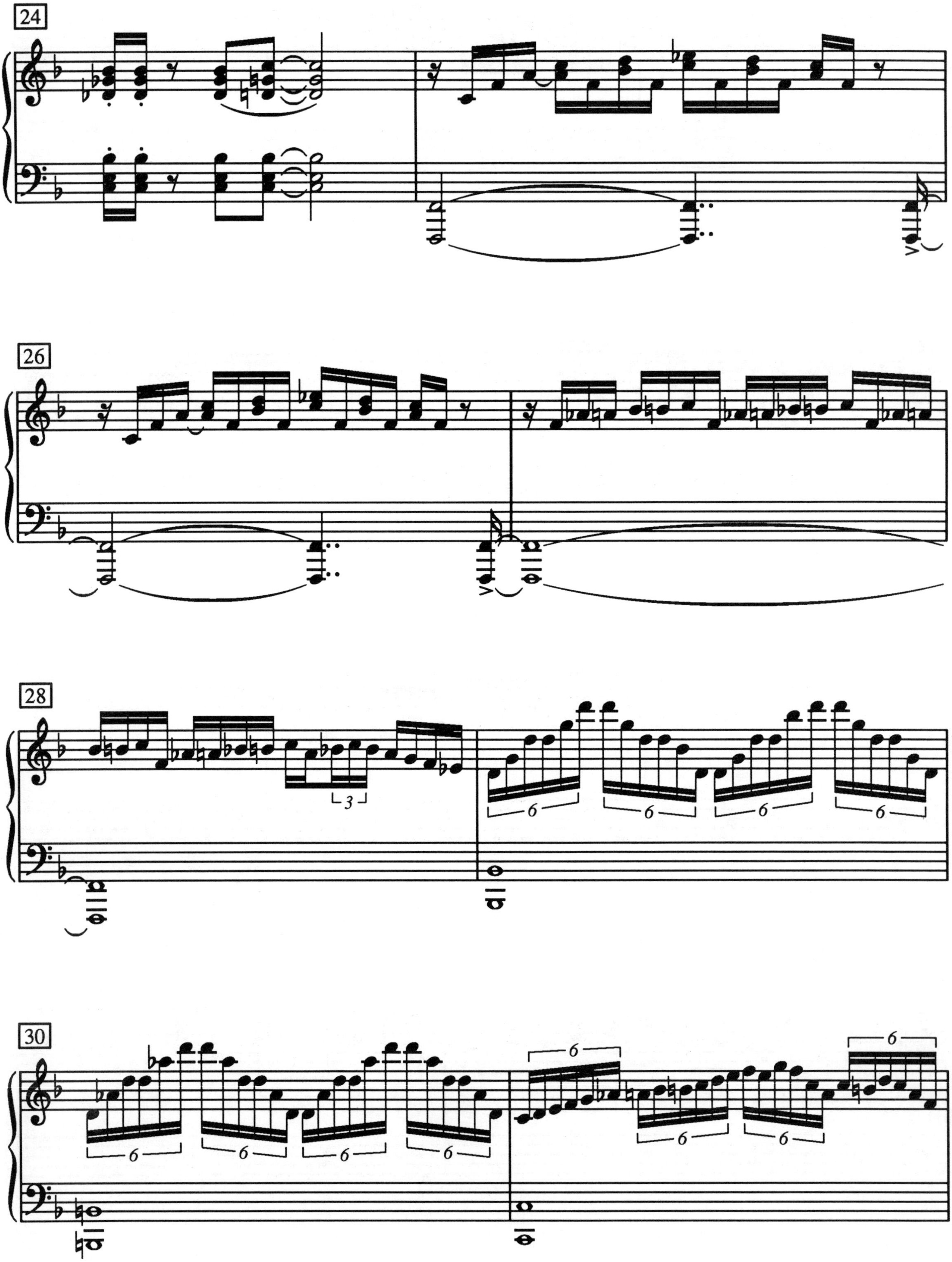
24
26
28
30

32
6
3
34
36
D. S. al Coda
CODA
38

Annette, My Pet

Composed and Arranged by
PAUL SMITH

13
16
19
22
D. S. 𝄋 al Coda
pp
RH
CODA
RH
LH
RH
f
p
LH
RH
LH
pp

Garnering the Blues

Composed and Arranged by
PAUL SMITH

14
Ab9
Bm7
E7
Am7
17
G7
20
GMaj7
G7
C7
Bbø
23
Bm7
Am7
G
Am7
26
Eb7
D7
G/D
Gø/D

29
G
Am7
Bm7
CMaj7
Bm7
Am7
G
G7
continuous roll octave
33
C9
F♯ø
C9
G
F♯
F
37
G
Bø
Am7
A♭7
41
G
Am7
Bm7
C6
GMaj7
roll
44
G7
C9
roll

47
GMaj7
Am7
50
CMaj7
Am7
B♭
C6
D. S. 𝄋 al Coda
CODA
G
Bø
Am7
C7
3
55
G
Bø
Am7
C7
3
G
Bø
58
Am7
C7
3
G
C
LH
C♯ø
G6

Improvising on the Blues

♩ = 88
Basic Melody

Composed and Arranged by
PAUL SMITH

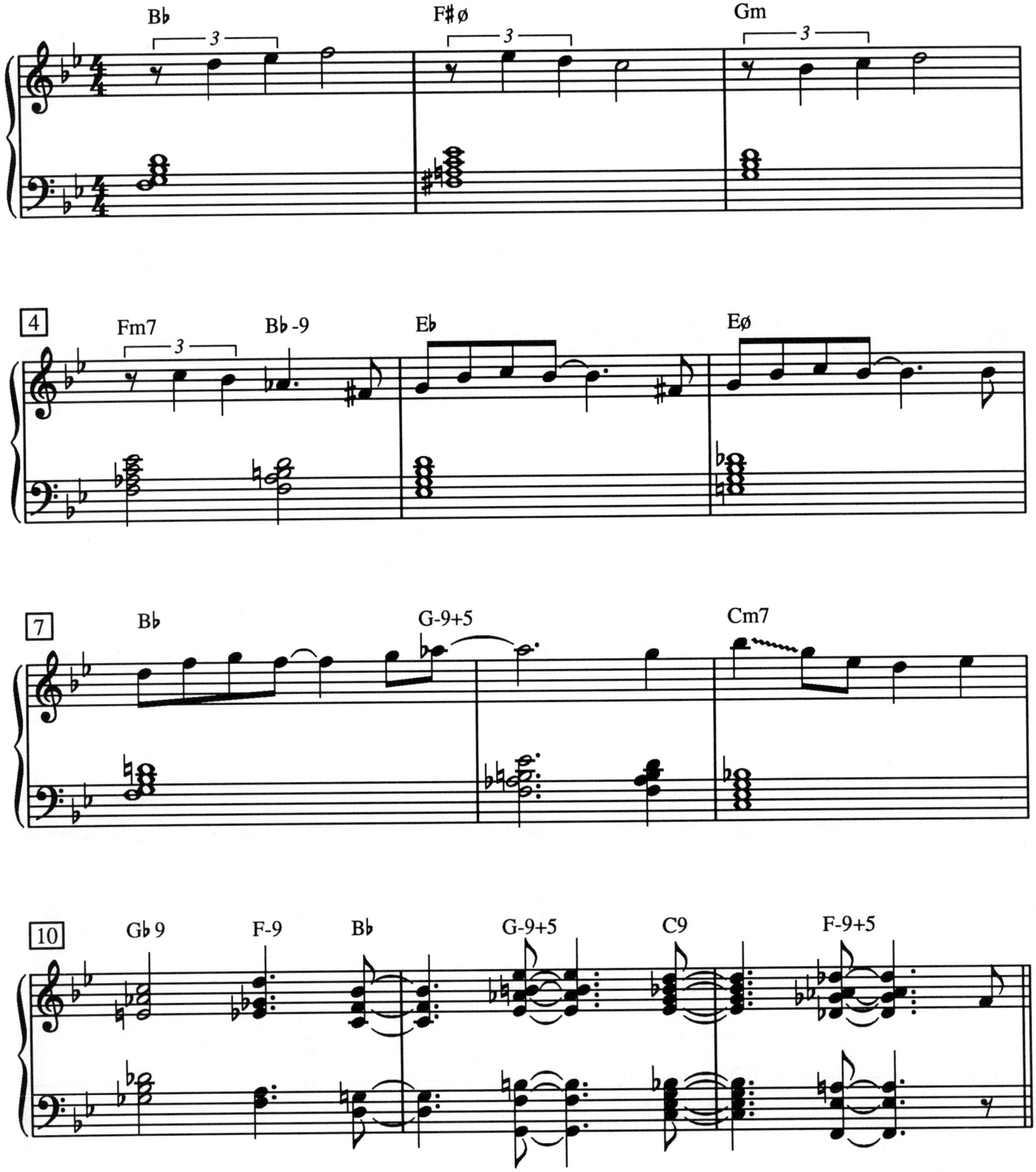

Improvised Chorus
13
B♭
F♯ø
Gm
16
Fm7
B♭ -9
E♭
Eø
19
B♭
G-9 -5
G7
Cm7
22
G♭ 9
F-9
B♭ Maj7
C-9 -5
Cm7
F-9 -5

25
Tag
Eb
Eø
Bb
28
Dm7-5
G9
Cm7
Ebm7
Ebm6
31
Bb
Bb Maj7
Fm6
G9
Eb
34
Cm7
rit.
Bb
Cb
Bb Maj7

Creative Keyboard Publications

MEL BAY

®